UNDERSTANDING AND IMPROVING

YOUR MENTAL HEALTH

BY

M. ASIF NAZIR

TABLE OF CONTENTS

AWARENESS OF MENTAL HEALTH

When most people think of health, they probably picture someone who is physically fit, has lots of energy, and is free from illness. But beyond this material world of health lies the intangible but no less important realm of mental health, which is poorly understood by the general public.

Definition of Mental Health

Contrary to popular belief, mental health does not simply refer to the absence of mental illness. It encompasses our mental, emotional, and social health. From early childhood to old age, our mental health has a significant impact on how we think, make wise decisions, connect with others, and handle stress. It's the bedrock upon which our happiness, resilience, and success in life rest.

The Influencing Factors

There are several interrelated factors that have an impact on our mental health. Our brain chemistry affects our emotions and thoughts, while our genes determine our susceptibility to certain diseases. Our upbringing, interpersonal experiences, and traumatic past all contribute to the uniqueness of our minds. Similarly, cultural norms and other social influences can have significant effects.

What Makes Comprehending So Important?

There are many benefits to learning about mental health. As a first step, it eliminates prejudice. Understanding the nuances of psychological health is a step towards eliminating stigma and discrimination. Second, education helps people learn to recognize the warning signs in themselves and others, which facilitates timely help and intervention.

Importance of Striking a Good Balance

Maintaining a healthy state of mind is essential, just as it is to value one's physical health. This equilibrium does not imply an indefinite state of bliss or the absence of sadness. Instead, it stands for overcoming obstacles, flourishing despite difficulties, and connecting with others in meaningful ways.

An Eternal Quest

Maintaining mental health is an ongoing process, not an end goal. The ups and downs of one's mental health may mirror the ups and downs of the external environment. Individuals can successfully negotiate these changes by increasing their knowledge, self-awareness, and access to appropriate resources.

GETTING AROUND IN YOUR FEELINGS

Emotions are like gold threads, interwoven throughout the human experience. These feelings, which can range from extreme happiness to crushing sadness, have a profound impact on our thoughts, deeds, and relationships. Emotions affect not only our mental health but also our relationships and the decisions we make in life, making it crucial that we learn to identify and manage them.

Emotional Spectrum's Widening

Imagine yourself on the coast of a huge ocean. Like the ocean, our internal landscape is constantly shifting, from calm to stormy and back to back again. Some feelings, like joy or sadness, are crystal clear, like the ocean near the shore. Deeper feelings, however, like the ocean's depths, may remain elusive, concealed by successive layers of awareness.

Tuning into the Currents

Understanding our emotions is the starting point of our journey. In the midst of the daily grind, it can be easy to ignore or bury our true feelings. Nonetheless, similar to ignoring the warning signs of an impending storm, ignoring our emotions can lead to tumultuous mental states. Understanding emotions calls for self-reflection and a heightened awareness of one's internal mental, physiological, and behavioral states.

Recognizing the Flows

There is always a reason why we feel a certain way. Anything from an external event, like a personal loss, to an internal thought process, like thinking or remembering, could fall into this category. Finding the origin of an emotion can help you gain perspective on why you're feeling it and better equip you to handle similar situations in the future.

Navigational Aids

After becoming aware of and familiar with our feelings, the next step is to learn how to handle, or navigate, them. This doesn't mean you have to stuff your feelings or force yourself to feel good. Instead, we're talking about how to react.

With the help of mindfulness and meditation, we can experience our feelings without becoming overwhelmed by them. Expressive outlets: writing, drawing, or even just talking to a friend can help release pent-up feelings. Exercise, yoga, or even just going for a walk are all great ways to release pent-up energy and refocus it in a positive direction. Help from an expert may be necessary if you feel overwhelmed by your emotions. Counselors and therapists can help by offering new insights, strategies, and techniques.

Emotional Life Interactions

Despite their inward focus, emotions have a noticeable effect on our relationships with others. Understanding and controlling our emotions is a key to effective communication, deeper connections, and greater compassion. In addition, our emotional state affects the decisions we make, whether they are minor or monumental.

Accepting the Journey

Finding emotional stability does not require a lack of turmoil. It's about learning to navigate rough waters, harnessing wind power, and staying on course when the going gets tough. In addition to ensuring our mental health, we can make the most of our lives by becoming more in tune with and controlling our feelings.

SIGNS OF MENTAL HEALTH ISSUES

Mental health is an integral part of the human experience, guiding us through the myriad obstacles we face every day. There are outward manifestations of mental health problems, just as there are outward manifestations of physical health problems. The key to ensuring one's health and happiness is knowing and recognizing these symptoms.

Mental health is not binary, consisting only of states of wellness or illness, but rather a nuanced spectrum. Everyone has bad days and feels down sometimes, but when those feelings last and have a significant impact on daily life, it may be a sign of something more serious. Mental health problems affect people of all ages and backgrounds to varying degrees. Depression, for instance, can show itself in a variety of ways, such as sadness, hopelessness, loss of interest in once-enjoyed activities, and even alterations in eating and sleeping habits. Excessive worry or fear, avoidance of certain places or activities, or intrusive thoughts are all symptoms that may accompany an anxiety disorder.

Mental health problems have complex and unique origins, but several risk factors tend to cluster together.

Genetics and chemical imbalances in the brain are just two examples of the biological factors that play a role. Traumatic experiences and past neglect, for example, can act as powerful triggers in their own right. Additionally, an individual may be more susceptible to similar challenges if they have a family history of mental health issues.

The breadth and depth of our feelings are intricately entwined with our general psychological well-being. Here, it's especially important to be able to tell the difference between fleeting emotions and more serious mental health issues. While it's normal to feel sad after suffering a significant loss, lingering melancholy could be a sign of something more serious.

When we go through life knowing these warning signs and the factors that contribute to them, we are better able to get help when we need it. This preventative method not only helps with the management of potential mental health obstacles but also creates a safe space for overall health and happiness.

STIGMATIZATION OF MENTAL ILLNESS

In every culture, certain subjects are off-limits for open discussion and open criticism. One such subject is mental health, which has not yet received the attention it deserves. Often, the genuine struggles that many people face every day are obscured by this veil of stigma, which is woven from misconceptions, myths, and societal prejudices. Initiating a progressive dialogue and correcting these misperceptions are not just acts of advocacy; they are essential to promoting tolerance and compassion in societies around the world.

Mental health issues have been interpreted differently by different cultures from the earliest times. They were considered curses by some, and spiritual or supernatural events by others. As knowledge in the medical field increased, people's views began to shift. The stigma attached to mental health is rooted in outdated ideas and widespread misinformation from the past.

Misconception number one: people with mental health problems are emotionally fragile. People who are struggling with these issues are often told to "toughen up" or "snap out of it," which only serves to reinforce the false notion that mental health problems are caused by a lack of willpower or resilience. These types of attitudes not only minimize real problems but also discourage people from getting help, which leads to more problems and more suffering.

As a result of this and similar myths, many people avoid talking about mental health and instead choose to suffer in silence. Recognizing, addressing, and discussing mental health concerns can pave the way to understanding, support, and recovery, just as it does with physical ailments.

Additionally, media portrayals of mental health frequently swing between idealizing and stigmatizing the topic. Misleading portrayals like these further muddle public comprehension by widening the gap between reality and perception. These depictions fuel stigma and make it harder for people who are struggling to open up about their experiences to do so.

However, there are signs of impending change. A more informed and compassionate society is slowly emerging as discussions about well-being enter the mainstream. Although gradual, this change is essential. Societies can advance toward complete health by dispelling harmful myths and creating spaces where people feel comfortable talking about their mental health.

Education is the cornerstone of progressive discourse. Education about mental health should be a standard part of school and community programs so that people of all ages have access to reliable resources. This information not only debunks myths but also equips people to recognize symptoms (in themselves and others) and seek treatment as soon as possible.

In addition, people with lived experience of mental health difficulties are critical to the process of narrative revision. By speaking out, they give faces to the problem, making it more than just a collection of numbers. Their stories of perseverance and hope can encourage others to speak up, starting a chain reaction that promotes mutual understanding and solidarity.

CONSTRUCTING RESISTANCE TO DISRUPTION

The unexpected turns of life frequently present us with tests of our mental and emotional fortitude. Our resilience and ability to withstand stress become most evident under these conditions. This ability, known as resilience, is not limited to a select few people but is instead a learned skill. Developing the ability to weather the storms of life is like building an umbrella that keeps us dry while still letting in the rain.

Self-confidence and the realization that difficulties are only temporary conditions are the bedrock of resilience. Those who have learned to harness their resilience view difficulties not as insurmountable, but as challenges to be met. As part of the human condition, they recognize and accept suffering, setbacks, and disillusionment. They don't let adversity define them, but rather, they use it to propel themselves forward.

The development of a strong social network is a cornerstone of resilience. As social beings, humans require interaction to feel fulfilled. Having people you can turn to for comfort, advice, and even just someone to listen to you when things get rough is invaluable. Simply talking about problems and putting them into words can help relieve some of the stress we're under.

It's important to cultivate an optimistic internal monologue in addition to receiving external support. How we deal with adversity depends on the stories we tell ourselves and the ones we choose to believe. Resilience can be fostered through the practice of challenging negative self-talk and replacing it with selfcompassionate and constructive thoughts.

Nonetheless, developing resilience is not the same as learning to stifle feelings. It's important to permit yourself to experience emotion. Understanding these feelings, working through them, and turning them into motivation are all essential components of resilience. It's about learning to direct your emotions constructively so that they can help rather than hurt. Setting attainable goals and taking some kind of action, even if it's just a small step, can help you feel more focused and motivated. Each accomplishment builds a stronger foundation upon which to stand. It's a reassuring reminder that our actions are within our control, even if we can't change the world around us. Furthe rmore, selfcare is critically important in building resilience. The indisputable connection between one's physical and mental health is why it is impossible to separate the two. Mental toughness can be greatly improved through practices like regular exercise, healthy eating, sufficient sleep, and relaxation methods like meditation and deep breathing exercises.

Constant change means there will always be obstacles to overcome. Both internal and external storms will buffet you along life's path. However, it is possible to not only survive but thrive in the face of adversity, by cultivating resilience and arming oneself with strategies to strengthen mental fortitude. Learning to dance in the rain, as the saying goes, is more important than waiting for the storm to pass. In this dance, resilience is our reliable partner, one who leads the way, lends a helping hand, and constantly affirms our inner fortitude.

THE REAL MEANING OF SELF-CARE

In recent years, "self-care" has become associated with spa days, indulgent treats, and relaxing vacations. These activities are important, but self-care goes deeper. True self-care nourishes the mind, body, and soul, improving mental health beyond fleeting indulgences.

Self-care involves intentional health care. It's a promise to prioritize well-being in the fast-paced modern world. Sustainable practices that promote long-term growth and healing are prioritized over fleeting pleasures.

Physical and mental health are essential to self-care. Mental fortitude is built on regular exercise, balanced nutrition, and adequate sleep. Yoga and meditation help connect physical and mental health by providing introspection and calm in a chaotic world.

Self-care goes beyond physical to emotional and psychological well-being. Set boundaries to protect mental space, take breaks to avoid burnout, and seek therapy or counseling when needed. Self-compassion—recognizing and honoring one's emotional needs without judgment or criticism—is essential to self-care.

In a tech-driven world, digital detoxification is a powerful self-care tool. Taking breaks from screens, social media, and the constant barrage of information can refresh and focus the mind. Deeper self- and worldconnections result from such breaks.

Authentic self-care includes relationship-building. Meaningful connections fuel humans' social lives. Spending time with family, friends, and support groups boosts emotional resilience. These bonds provide stability, understanding, and belonging.

Self-care includes personal development and learning. Activities that challenge the mind and spark passion and curiosity give purpose and fulfillment. A new hobby, skill, or thought-provoking book stimulates the mind and enriches it.

Please note that self-care is not a one-size-fits-all concept. What energizes one may drain another. A journey of self-discovery and introspection. It involves acknowledging needs, setting boundaries, and following one's path to well-being.

MEDITATION AND REFLECTION

Amidst the noise and chaos of today's fast-paced world, with its never-ending stimuli and unrelenting demands, there is a peaceful haven that welcomes all who enter. This haven of peace and tranquility has been around for millennia, and it is the home of meditation and awareness. Despite their ancient origins, these rituals continue to play an important role in modern society by providing comfort to the weary and insight to the confused.

Simply put, mindfulness is the act of bringing one's full attention and focus to the here and now. It's the ability to take in information without filtering it through one's own opinions or biases. In this heightened state of consciousness, the ghosts of the past and the unknowns of the future vanish, and only the pure, unadulterated essence of the present remains.

Mindfulness and meditation are two practices that explore the inner workings of the mind in greater depth. It's an intentional act, a journey into oneself, to reachto reach beyond the surface of things to the depths of one's being. Meditation helps people achieve balance, where inner peace triumphs over external chaos, through techniques like deep breathing, chanting, and silent reflection.

These practices have transformative potential because they help to bring one's attention inward, away from external stimuli, and into harmony with one's true nature. When everything is in harmony, stress, anxiety, and negative emotions typically fade away, and a serene calm takes its place. An uncluttered and clear mind is more open and sensitive to life's nuances, fostering greater innovation, compassion, and health.

The popularity of contemplative practices like meditation and mindfulness has skyrocketed in this age of constant stimulation from screens both real and virtual. Information overload and constant connectivity can make people feel disoriented and detached from their surroundings and from who they are as individuals. Mindfulness shines as a lighthouse in this cacophony, centering people and prompting them to reflect on the preciousness and transience of the present moment.

The analytical eye of contemporary science has also begun to investigate and verify the efficacy of these time-honored methods. Consistent practice of mindfulness and meditation has been shown to alter brain structure, improving memory, empathy, and executive decision-making while attenuating regions linked to stress and anxiety. These results highlight the significant influence these habits have on both mental and physical health.

The changes to neural pathways and brain structures are beneficial, but there is also a deeper, more intangible shift. Mindfulness and meditation practitioners frequently report feeling more at one with themselves and the universe. When one experiences a spiritual awakening, they feel a renewed sense of meaning, fulfillment, and happiness because they know they are a part of something greater than themselves.

As the world speeds ahead with technological wonders and constant innovations, the appeal of the past only increases. The ancient practices of mindfulness and meditation call to the hearts of today's seekers in search of solace and insight. When two people embrace, they learn not only about the present but also about the eternal truths of life.

FOUNDATIONAL RELATIONSHIPS

Relationships emerge as colorful threads in the intricate tapestry that is the human experience, weaving together patterns of happiness and sadness, trust and betrayal. They range from the euphoric highs of love and friendship to the desolate lows of conflict and estrangement. They cover the entire spectrum of human emotion. These relationships, whether they are familial, romantic, platonic, or professional, play a pivotal role in the formation of our lives. They serve as pillars that either support our mental well-being or contribute to the strain that it is under, depending on how we choose to view them.

The human psyche, with its intricate dance of thoughts and feelings, is always on the lookout for connections. The infant forms a bond with the primary caregiver from the very beginning of their lives, laying the groundwork for a foundation of trust and security. People tend to cultivate relationships as they move through the various stages of life because they are looking for companionship, understanding, and validation from those around them. These connections, when fostered with care and respect, have the potential to act as anchors and provide a sense of security in a world that is fraught with uncertainty.

The development of healthy relationships with other people has the potential to improve one's mental health in a variety of different ways. They provide individuals with emotional support and serve as safe havens where people can share their fears, aspirations, joys, and sorrows. Simply being able to talk to someone you trust and confide in can help alleviate feelings of isolation during times of crisis and reinforce the belief that you are not alone. A sense of belonging, a community in which individuals are made to feel that they are valued and accepted, is another benefit of having healthy relationships. This sense of inclusion can help strengthen self-esteem, which in turn can foster a positive image of oneself.

On the other hand, the same bonds can place a significant amount of strain on one's mental health when they are fraught with negativity or conflict. Feelings of entrapment, anxiety, and a diminished sense of one's self-worth can be the result of relationships that are marked by manipulation, distrust, or abuse. These bonds, rather than providing solace, become sources of stress, which in turn exacerbate feelings of loneliness and desolation in the individual. The emotional toll of navigating troubled relationships can manifest itself in a variety of different ways, ranging from changes in mood and quality of sleep to more serious issues related to mental health. Connections made in the workplace and the community also have a bearing on one's mental health; this is in addition to the effect that personal relationships have. It is possible to improve one's level of happiness at work and in life as a whole by cultivating a supportive work environment that is characterized by understanding, collaboration, and respect. On the other hand, mental peace can be eroded by toxic workplace dynamics, which are characterized by competition, harassment, or excessive stress. This can lead to burnout and dissatisfaction. In the broader context of society as a whole, the feeling of being connected to a larger whole and of being a part of a community both play an important role in an individual's overall mental health. Individuals are provided with an opportunity for selfexpression, participation in meaningful activities, and personal development when community bonds are formed through the cultivation of shared interests, cultural practices, or societal initiatives. Volunteering, attending cultural events, or even just participating in neighborhood initiatives are all examples of activities that can help foster a sense of purpose and belonging in a community, which can help mitigate feelings of alienation or isolation.

In conclusion, the human psyche is profoundly affected by relationships in all of their varied manifestations. They are capable of elevating, healing, and nurturing others, but they also have the potential to hurt, harm, and hinder others. It is of the utmost importance to acknowledge the part that these connections play in one's mental health. It is imperative to cultivate and tend to positive relationships while simultaneously establishing boundaries to protect oneself from toxic relationships and conflict. Individuals not only discover the joys of companionship but also the strength to navigate the challenges that life presents, drawing solace from the connections that truly matter when they find themselves in this delicate balance.

SETTING LIMITS SAYING 'NO'

An often-overlooked yet crucial skill emerges amid the balancing act of roles, responsibilities, and relationships: the ability to set limits. Even something as seemingly innocuous as setting boundaries can have significant effects on one's mental health. In addition to recognizing the worth of one's own time, energy, and emotional space, learning to say "no" is also about learning to say "yes" to oneself.

The idea of boundaries extends far beyond the merely physical to the spheres of the mind and the computer. These boundaries that people create for themselves are meant to keep them safe from harm, exploitation, and stress. They represent self-respect and the will to protect oneself from harm.

However, it's common to encounter internal and external resistance when attempting to establish boundaries. Such behavior could be deemed inconsiderate, rigid, and even selfish depending on the observer's upbringing, culture, and worldview. People may not speak up for themselves for fear of being rejected or judged, and as a result, they may forego their own needs to please or fit in. In doing so, however, they end up devaluing their own needs, which can lead to feelings of resentment, burnout, and emotional exhaustion.

The first step in realizing the importance of boundaries is looking inward. Understanding one's limitations, strengths, and needs is essential. Everyone has their capacity to handle pressure, dedication, and social interaction. Some people may do better in busy social settings, while others prefer quieter ones. While some people enjoy being able to juggle multiple tasks at once, others might find that distracting. The first step in creating healthy boundaries is realizing there are subtle differences.

After acceptance, the next obstacle is to assert oneself. It takes courage to say "no," especially to those you care about or in a professional setting. However, it's crucial to set limits in a way that's clear, firm, and, most importantly, guilt-free. While this claim may be met with resistance or surprise at first, it ultimately lays the groundwork for mutual respect and comprehension. When people are consistent in setting and maintaining limits, their environments change to accommodate them.

In addition, digital boundaries become increasingly important in today's age of pervasive digital media and virtual interactions that blur the lines between the private and the public. Setting aside time to relax, unplug from the never-ending stream of notifications, and take planned breaks from the digital world can help refresh the mind and restore concentration.

Boundaries can be used as a tool for introspection and development. Dedicating time to activities like reading, meditation, crafting, or even just resting demonstrates a commitment to one's well-being. It serves as a gentle yet firm reminder that one's health and happiness are important, even amidst the din of obligations and responsibilities.

DEVELOPING A LONG-TERM MENTAL HEALTH PLAN

Through the course of our lives, we encounter a wide range of emotions and situations, some of which are more pleasant than others. As we move through this ever-changing landscape, having a map, a guide to help us negotiate the complexities of mental health, becomes crucial. Developing a long-term strategy for mental health and resilience can serve as this map, a lighthouse pointing the way to complete wellness.

Introspection proves invaluable at the outset of this endeavor. Meditation is the practice of pausing from one's busy life to assess one's emotional and mental health in the present moment. It's about taking stock of feelings, making observations, and pinpointing problem areas. The cornerstones of a long-term strategy for mental health and wellness can be built upon the solid groundwork laid by this introspection.

After taking some time for personal reflection, the focus should shift to learning and raising consciousness. It's about being well-versed in the subject of mental health, with an appreciation for its complexity and awareness of the many factors that can affect it. Knowledge of the mind and how to keep it healthy can be gained through reading, workshops, seminars, and professional counseling.

Now that we have this information, we can shift our attention to applying it. Here, knowledge from various fields comes together to help shape an all-encompassing approach to emotional health. Depending on the individual, this plan may include anything from self-care rituals and boundary-setting techniques to mindfulness training and psychiatric consultation.

The importance of one's social life to their overall health should be obvious. Building strong bonds with others becomes crucial because they provide psychological sustenance and a feeling of belonging. On the flip side, it is equally important to recognize and separate from relationships that are toxic or draining.

Additionally, in this technological age, setting digital boundaries is crucial. Setting aside time to unplug, reduce your screen time, and participate in offline activities can provide a welcome break from the onslaught of digital information and help you focus and unwind.

The indisputable link between physical and mental health is reason enough to include it in this allencompassing strategy. Mental fortitude and resilience can be greatly bolstered by engaging in regular physical activity, eating a balanced diet, getting plenty of sleep, and practicing relaxation techniques like deep breathing or meditation.

However, coming up with a strategy is only the first step. The real difficulty will come from making sure it's always followed. It entails making a deliberate effort to care for oneself, giving one's mental health top priority despite one's busy schedule. It's important to go back and tweak the plan every so often to make sure it still fits your current situation.

Finally, keep in mind that failures are inevitable along the way. There could be times of uncertainty, relapse, or emotional upheaval. However, rather than signifying failure, these temporary setbacks provide openings for development, education, and re-evaluation. As a person faces and overcomes adversity, their mental health and wellness plan evolves to become more comprehensive and tailored to their specific path.

In conclusion, taking the initiative to create a long-term strategy for mental health is an act of love, respect, and protection for oneself. It's an all-encompassing method that, while being realistic about the difficulties, looks ahead with optimism to forge a course toward perseverance, development, and long-term emotional wellness.